Auschwitz...
Auschwitz...

Belzec...
Belzec...

Sobibor...
Sobibor...

Treblinka...
Treblinka...

Majdanek...
Majdanek...

Kulmhof am Ner...
Kulmhof am Ner...

German concentration and extermination camps

The first concentration camps in Germany were created in 1933 after the Nazis came to power. These camps were used by them to isolate their political opponents or people whose activity was considered subversive for the state. After war broke out in 1939 the Nazis created camps in the territories of occupied Poland and other occupied countries. The purpose of these concentration camps was extermination. Inside them the Nazis created terrible living conditions with the sole purpose of causing a high death rate amongst the prisoners. An important function of these camps was also the economic exploitation of those imprisoned who were used as slave labour for certain branches of the German economy. The German Nazis considered some of the nations in occupied Europe as inferior races, with the result that they selected Poles and eastern Slavs to be gradually eradicated and their lands settled by Germans. The Jews and the Gypsies were selected for immediate extermination. After they were brought to the camp, the Jews were sent directly to the gas chambers where they were killed. In the occupied areas the Nazis created six extermination camps within the borders of pre-war Poland: Kulmhof in Chełm on Ner, Bełżec, Sobibór, Treblinka, Auschwitz in Oświęcim and Majdanek in Lublin. The latter two functioned also as concentration camps. Another concentration camp was created in Płaszów. Within the territory of present day Poland there are also the former camps, Gross Rosen in Rogoźnica and Stutthof in Sztutowo. The biggest of all the camps enumerated was Auschwitz, to which between 1940 and 1945 the German Nazis transported 1,1 million Jews, 140-150 thousand Poles, 23 thousand Gypsies, 15 thousand prisoners of war from the Soviet Union and 25 thousand prisoners of other nationalities.

GERMAN
PLACES OF
EXTERMINATION
IN POLAND

Auschwitz

Belzec

Sobibor

Treblinka

Majdanek

Kulmhof am Ner

Auschwitz as a concentration camp

In 1939 the western area of Poland, including Oświęcim was incorporated into the III Reich. The Germans changed the name of the town to Auschwitz and created the concentration camp in the spring of 1940. It was built on the site of former Polish Army barracks on the outskirts of the town of Oświęcim, near large railway sidings connecting the town to other parts of Poland. This location facilitated the transport of prisoners and isolated them from the outside world as those inhabitants living near the camp were also relocated. Konzentrationslager (KL) Auschwitz was – as were the other concentration camps – a state-run institution financed by the German state budget. On June 14, 1940 the German authorities sent the first transport to KL Auschwitz from the prison in Tarnów which consisted of 728 Polish prisoners and from that moment Poles were sent to the camp until the autumn of 1944. After the Jews, Poles were the second group of prisoners and victims of the camp – between 70 and 75 thousand of them were murdered here. From 1941 the German Nazis started to deport other occupied countries citizens to the camp. During the time the camp was functioning around 1.1 million Jews, 150 thousand Poles, 23 thousand Gypsies, 15 thousand prisoners of war from the Soviet Union and 25 thousand prisoners of other nation were sent to the camp. Most of them were killed there.

In 1941 the SS authorities began expanding KL Auschwitz with the construction of another camp in the adjacent village Brzezinka (Birkenau). The inhabitants of the few adjacent villages were first removed. In 1942 close to the chemical plant under construction and property of the German company, IG-Farbenindustrie, the third camp named Buna was created. In 1943 KL Auschwitz was divided into three camps: the original camp Auschwitz I, Auschwitz II-Birkenau in the area of village Brzezinka and Auschwitz III, which controlled Buna and sub-camps created next to industrial plants, mainly in Silesia and the western part of Małopolska.

In 1942 the Nazis started to send women to Auschwitz who constituted about 30 per cent of all prisoners registered in the camp (131.560 female prisoners) and half of the victims murdered in the gas chambers right after their arrival in the camp. In 1942 the first transport of children with families came to the camp. They were mostly Jewish children but included Polish, Gypsies, and Belorussians. In total 232 thousand children and youngsters were deported. The horrific living conditions in Auschwitz were the main cause of the high death rate. Prisoners died from starvation and the rapid spread of diseases because of the terrible living conditions and the work they were forced to do. SS doctors put prisoners through medical experiments which killed or crippled them for life. The SS punished the prisoners severely for the slightest offence. They beat prisoners brutally and thousands were executed – firing squads, hangings or killed with phenol injections during experiments. The executions by firing squads, carried out mainly on Poles – took place in front of the 'Death Wall' in Auschwitz I. This camp contained a gas chamber and crematorium I. Here, Jews from the first transports, prisoners from the Soviet Union as well as the sick and the elderly were murdered by the SS.

Auschwitz as a place of Jewish extermination

On January 20, 1942, fifteen high-ranking Nazi party and German government leaders gathered for an important meeting at the Wannsee Conference. This meeting with key non-SS government leaders, including the secretaries of the Foreign Ministry and Justice, whose cooperation was needed was held for the purpose of discussing the 'final solution to the Jewish question in Europe'. The plan was the extermination of all the Jews living in Europe – the number estimated by the German officials was at over 11 million. And these Jewish people were murdered by the Nazis in the places of extermination they constructed for this purpose. By 1944 Auschwitz II-Birkenau was the largest of them. Between 1942 and 1944 the Nazis brought to Auschwitz: 1.1 million Jews from: Hungary (approx. 438 thousand), Poland (approx. 300 thousand), France (approx. 69 thousand), the Netherlands (approx. 60 thousand), Greece (approx. 55 thousand), Moravia and Czechy (approx. 46 thousand), Belgium (approx. 60 thousand), Slovakia (approx. 27 thousand), Germany and Austria (approx. 23 thousand), Yugoslavia (approx. 10 thousand), Italy (approx. 7,5 thousand), Latvia (approx. one thousand), Norway (690 people) and other camps (approx. 34 thousand). From those deported the Nazis murdered close to one million people. In most cases, people were transported to Auschwitz in cattle wagons, the journey lasting several days. Most of the transported Jews thought they were going to be relocated to new places where they would settle and start a new life. Until May of 1944 the trains stopped next to the ramp at the end of the railway line between Auschwitz I and Auschwitz II-Birkenau. When the ramp in Birkenau was completed the trains stopped there. The people were off-loaded from the cattle wagons and the women and children were lined up in one column and men in another. SS doctors made the selection on the ramps sentencing most of the people to death. A few were considered healthy or strong enough to work and were sent to the camp. The remaining 70 per cent were taken by the SS directly to the gas chambers. In 1942 in Birkenau the gas chambers were in deserted Polish houses adapted for this purpose. From the spring of 1943 the gas chambers and crematoria were situated in four newly constructed buildings. When the people arrived at the gas chambers (they were not aware of its function) they were told to undress in the changing rooms by SS guards and then led to a gas chamber resembling a bathhouse. After the doors were closed and locked the SS guards

Auschwitz

poured granules of poison into the gas chamber. As these granules came into contact with the warm air they broke down into a deadly, poisonous gas causing slow asphyxiation. When the SS guards were sure that everyone inside was dead the doors to the gas chamber were opened and the Sonnderkommadno prisoners started their work. This group of workers, made up of mainly Jews had now to move the bodies out of the gas chamber, then cut their hair, pull out any teeth made of gold or silver and transport the bodies to the crematoriums where they were burnt or thrown into large pits inside of which a fire was burning. The Sonnderkommadno prisoners also had to grind down any remaining bones in the ashes of the cremated corpses. This ash was later transported by trucks by the SS to be dumped in rivers, ponds or as fertilizer onto fields belonging to the camp farms. According to Nazi ideology Gypsies were also sent to Auschwitz were like the Jews the majority of them were exterminated. The last group of Gypsies was murdered in the gas chambers on August 2, 1944 during the demolition of the 'Gypsy camp' in Auschwitz II-Birkenau. There are cases of prisoners of different nationalities who, despite the continuous menace of death tried to oppose the camp authorities. They formed secret organizations, some of which kept in touch with the Polish resistance in the vicinity of the camp. This underground resistance movement provided the prisoners with food, medicine and helped in escapes. They also transmitted messages about the situation in the camp to the outside world, for example, in September 1944 a secret radio station in Poland sent a telegram to London informing them that the SS authorities were planning to close down the camp and murder all the prisoners in the camp. At the request of the Polish Cabinet, the British and American governments made these plans public in the declaration of October 10, 1944, with a warning that the perpetrators of the genocide would be punished. As a result the SS authorities stopped the plan from being carried out. They did not stop, however, their plans to execute the Sonderkommando group of several hundred prisoners. On the October 7, 1944 those who had been selected for extermination rebelled in Birkenau. They destroyed one crematorium and continued the fight against the SS, killing three SS guards and wounding a dozen or so. During the process of quashing the uprising the SS killed 250 prisoners and another 200 after the uprising was put down. It was the only armed rebellion in KL Auschwitz. At the end of 1944 the SS began dismantling and destroying the gas chambers, crematoria and other facilities, as well as documents, in Auschwitz II-Birkenau.

On the 17th January 1945 the evacuation of about 58 000 prisoners to be marched deep into the territory of the III Reich began. Most of the evacuated prisoners died or were killed by the SS guards during the 'March of Death'. When Red Army soldiers entered the camp on January 27 they found about 7000 mostly sick and dying prisoners. On July 2, 1947 in accordance with the act of the Sejm the National Museum Oświęcim-Brzezinka (Auschwitz-Birkenau) was created in the two remaining parts of Auschwitz I and Auschwitz II-Birkenau. The victims of the camps are remembered by the plaques and memorials in the area of the former camp complex and its 22 sub-camps. The largest of these memorials is the International Monument erected in 1967 to commemorate those who died in Auschwitz II-Birkenau. Their memory is also preserved by exhibitions, scientific research and publishing activities, as well as gatherings in memory of the victims organized on anniversaries of the first transport of Poles to the camp, the liquidation of the gypsy camp and the liberation of the camp. During the annual March of the Living young Jewish people leave plaques with the names of the Holocaust victims in the camp.

The main entrance to Auschwitz I. On June 14 and 20, 1940 the German Nazis sent the first transports of Polish political detainees from prisons in Tarnów and Nowy Wiśnicz to the concentration camp in Auschwitz. In the summer of that year, during the replacement of the provisionally installed fence with a permanent one, the Wiśnicz prisoners constructed the gate on top of which is the inscription 'Arbeit macht Frei' – 'Work liberates' (photograph from 1945 by Stanisław Łuczko).

Auschwitz I. Prisoners digging and building the camp kitchen. This forced hard labour under the SS led to the death of many prisoners and this type of work was one of the components of the extermination plan. Many prisoners worked on the demolition of the buildings left by the displaced Poles and Jews, on the construction of barracks in the camp and the adjacent arable, cattle and fish farms, belonging to it. From 1942 inmates were used in the construction, near Oświęcim, of the 'Buna' chemical plant belonging to the well-known German company, I. G. Farbenindustrie, as well as in mines, foundries and factories mainly in the western parts of the Małopolska region and Upper Silesia (SS photograph).

← Auschwitz I. The barracks in the camp were surrounded by a double fence made of reinforced concrete poles with electrified, high tension, barb wire attached to them. In addition a high concrete wall was built along the two roads situated near the camp. It was supposed to hide the camp from the prying eyes of the outside world (photograph from 1945 by Stanisław Mucha).

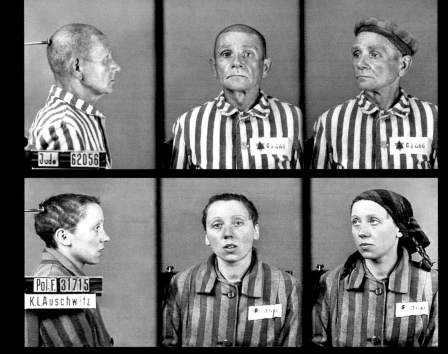

Photographs of people taken during their registration in the camp. Poles were the first to be imprisoned and murdered in KL Auschwitz. From 1941 the German Nazis brought other countries' citizens to the camp and in 1942 women were sent to the camp for the first time (SS photograph).

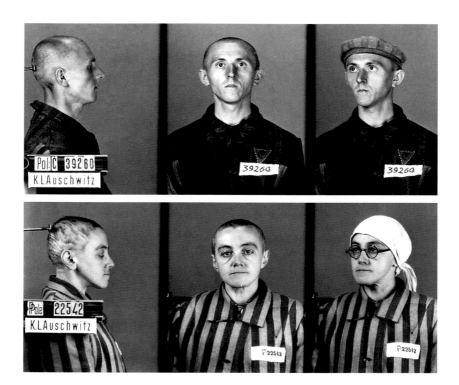

People were given numbers to replace their names. The capital letter before the number denoted their nationality: P for Poles, F for French, R for Russians, C for Czechs and Z for Gypsies. The letters were placed on various coloured triangles, e.g. red denoted political detainees. The Star of David, denoting Jews, was formed from two triangles, one of them turned upside down (SS photograph).

Auschwitz I. 'The Death Wall' in front of which mainly Poles and other nationalities were executed by the SS. Block 11 (on the right) called 'the Death Block' contained the cells in which prisoners were put as punishment or because the camp Gestapo were investigating them. In its cellars the SS committed the first mass murder using Zyklon B. During the first, 'test run' they killed Soviet prisoners of war and the sick (photograph taken after the war by Stanisław Mucha).

The gas chamber and the crematorium I in Auschwitz I. The crematorium functioned from August 15, 1940. According to experiments by the German authorities, 340 corpses could be burnt in it over a period of 24 hours. In the autumn of 1941 the largest room in the building was adapted as a gas chamber. Here the SS, using Zyklon B, killed Jews, Soviet prisoners of war and the sick whom the SS doctors selected as unable for further work. The chamber was closed down in July 1943 because four other gas chambers and crematoria had been built in Auschwitz II Birkenau (photograph taken after the war by Lidia Foryciarz).

The displacement by the Germans of Polish families from the village of Brzezinka. Two years later, not far from here, the Nazis built the gas chambers and the crematoria IV and V. During 1940 and 1941 the German authorities displaced from the region several thousand Poles and Jews living in Oświęcim and adjacent villages (photograph from 1941 taken secretly by a Brzezinka resident, Augustyn Gładyszek).

BIRKENAU EXTERMINATION COMPLEX
OSWIECIM, POLAND
31 MAY 1944

EXECUTION AREA

"LOOT" STORAGE
B-III

SECURITY SCREEN

SMOKE

RAILCARS

TRENCHES

BIB

TRENCHES

WOMEN'S CAMP

PRISONER'S HOSPITAL (B-IIF)

BIA

GYPSY CAMP (B-IIE)

MEN'S CAMP (B-IID)

HUNGARIAN CAMP (B-IIC)

SECURITY SCREEN

FAMILY CAMP (B-IIB)

B-III SECTION

QUARANTINE CAMP (B-IIA)

15

Arial photo of Auschwitz II-Birkenau taken on May 31, 1944 by American air reconnaissance. In the autumn of 1941 the camp authorities started the construction of a new camp in the fields of the deserted village of Brzezinka. The camp was systematically developed during the following years. It consisted of three parts, the sections B I (on the left), the largest – B II (in the center) and the never completed – B III (on the right). In the spring of 1944 between sections B I and B II a siding was created at the end of which the gas chambers and crematoria II and III were situated. In the right upper corner of the section B II were gas chambers and crematoria IV and V.

Auschwitz II-Birkenau. The wooden barracks in section B II (photograph from 1945).

Auschwitz II-Birkenau. Female prisoners inside the wooden barracks. The living conditions inside were appalling. →
The wooden barracks were created for 400 prisoners; but in most cases they held many more.
Because of overcrowding and the lack of the necessary sanitary facilities the barracks were infested
with vermin and rats (photograph by a Soviet soldier after the liberation of the camp).

Auschwitz II-Birkenau. The main gate called 'The Death Gate', through which, from the spring of 1944, transports of Jews passed. In August and September of that year they were joined by transports of Warsaw inhabitants. (photograph from 1945 by J. Frąckiewicz).

Auschwitz II-Birkenau. The building of gas chamber and crematorium V which functioned from March 1943. The holes through which the SS guards dropped the granules of Zyklon B were situated inside the wall of the gas chamber. According to the German authorities 768 corpses could be burnt in crematorium V over a period of 24 hours (SS photograph).

Auschwitz II-Birkenau. The furnace hall in crematorium II. After the gas chambers were opened the Sonderkommando prisoners, under the supervision of the SS, brought out the corpses, cut their hair, pulled out their gold teeth and transported them to the furnaces in which they were to be burnt (SS photograph).

Hungarian Jews on the loading ramp of Auschwitz II-Birkenau just before the selection – the SS placed women with children on one side and men on the other. Most of them would be sentenced to death by SS doctors. In the background the 'The Death Gate' is visible and the barracks of section B I of the women's camp (SS photograph 1944).

Hungarian Jews just after disembarkation from wagons onto the ramp in Auschwitz II-Birkenau. → Visible in the distance, to the left of the railway siding, is the gas chamber building and Crematorium No. II. (SS photograph 1944).

Auschwitz II-Birkenau. A group of Jewish women from Hungary, with their children, on their way to the gas chamber. In the background gas chamber and crematorium III buildings are visible. During the selection SS doctors sentenced to death the majority of Jews from each transport. People of advanced age, the disabled and women with children had no chance of surviving the selection (SS photography 1944).

Auschwitz II-Birkenau. The last moments before entering the gas chamber. In the background gas chamber and crematorium IV buildings are visible (SS photograph 1944).

Auschwitz II-Birkenau. Women and children before entering the changing room adjacent to gas chamber IV. In the background the camp storage houses are visible. Belongings taken from the deported Jews were stored here (SS photograph 1944).

Doors from gas chamber II or III. Before the gas chambers and crematoria were blown up by the SS the doors were removed. (After the war they were found in the area of the camp). As soon as the Jews were inside the gas chamber the doors, in which there was a glass spy hole, were locked by the SS guards with double iron catches, bolted together (photograph from 1945 by Stanisław Łuczko).

A can containing Zyklon B granules. The SS guards poured the granules into the gas chamber filled with people. →
When these granules came into contact with warm air they emitted a deadly, poisonous gas (photograph from 1957).

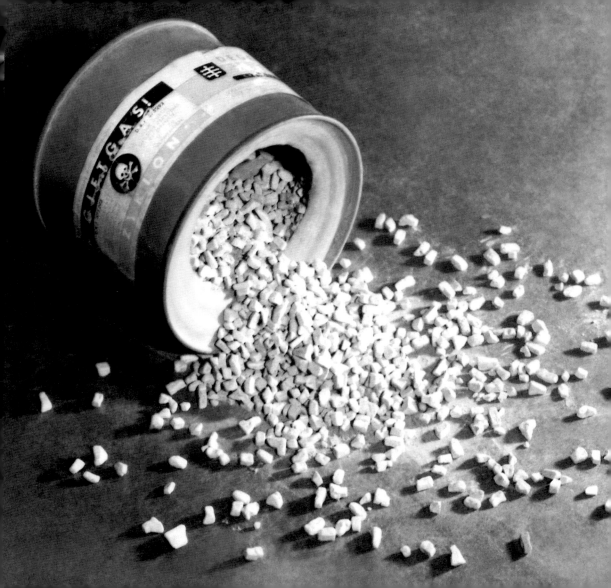

Partially burnt remains of victims in Auschwitz II-Birkenau (photograph taken
by a Soviet soldier after the liberation of the camp in 1945).

Auschwitz II-Birkenau. The burning storage
sheds filled with Jewish belongings after
the liberation of the camp – end of January
1945. From autumn 1944 the SS started
to cover up the evidence of the genocide
they had committed here. Documents were
burnt and gas chambers and crematoria
demolished. In January 1945 when
the Red Army was near the SS blew up
the crematoria and set the camp storage
sheds on fire (photography by a Soviet
soldier in January 1945).

The inside of one of the wooden barracks in the former Auschwitz II-Birkenau camp (contemporary photograph).

A watchtower in the former Auschwitz II-Birkenau camp (contemporary photograph).

The 'Death Gate' in the former Auschwitz II-Birkenau camp (contemporary photograph).

Penal company prisoners at work. A part of a drawing by → an unknown prisoner found on the wall of Block I in the former Auschwitz II-Birkenau camp (contemporary photograph).

The entrance gate and some
of the buildings of the former Auschwitz I
camp (contemporary photograph).

The Belzec extermination camp was created in the Kozielsk Hill region and building commenced on November 1, 1941. It was the first 'instant death' concentration camp created for the implementation of 'Operation Reinhard' – the aim of which was the extermination of the Jews in the General Government zone of the III Reich. It was also the first camp in which the Nazis used stationary gas chambers to exterminate people, benefiting from the experience acquired during the Euthanasia Program carried out in Germany, where mentally ill patients were killed in gas chambers. The first transport came to the Belzec camp on March 17, 1942. The Belzec prisoners came mainly from the ghettos of Lublin and Lvov. By the middle of April 1942 about 60 000 Jews from Lublin and the Galicia district had been murdered in these primitive gas chambers. Another wave of transports was directed to the camp in May and June of that year. This time the prisoners also came from the Kraków district, mostly Kraków and Tarnów. Between June and July the camp was rebuilt. The Germans built larger, concrete gas chambers able to exterminate up to 4000 people at once. The second phase in the operation of the camp was characterized by the inflow of larger transports from the area south of Lublin as well as from the Kraków and Galicia districts. By the middle of December 1942 Bełżec had become the mass grave for Jews from Lublin, Lwów, Kraków, Rzeszów, Tarnów, Przemyśl, Stanisławów, Tarnopol, Drohobycz and hundreds of adjacent small towns. During 9 months in 1942 transports brought about 500 000 Jews to be murdered in Bełżec. They were mostly Jews from Poland; with some of the victims also from countries such as: Germany, Austria, the Czech Republik and Slovakia. These people had been deported previously by the Germans to temporary ghettos, mainly in the Lublin district. Bełżec was considered by the Nazi Germans as an experimental camp. The whole procedure of dealing with the victims was organized here and tried out in this camp and these procedures were used later in other extermination camps, namely Sobibor and Treblinka, during 'Operation Reinhard'. In Bełżec there was no selection. All the transported Jews were escorted to the dressing rooms. They had to leave all their personal belongings there as well as their money and other valuables. Men were sent to the gas chambers first, then the women and children. Women had their hair cut just before they were sent to die in the gas chambers. The cause of death in the chambers was asphyxiation from the exhaust fumes of captured Soviet tank petrol engines. The fumes were supplied to the chambers by a system of pipes. The whole process of killing in the gas chamber took from 20 to 30 minutes. The bodies were then piled into mass graves. In Bełżec there were 33 of these graves. The camp as such was not very large as it only covered an area of little more than 7 hectares (17.3 acres). It was divided into two parts. The first part contained the barracks in which the guards, former Soviet prisoners who had gone over to the side of the Germans, lived. This part also included the storage and maintenance barracks as well as the changing rooms and the ramp, where the transports arrived. The second part was the actual death camp with the gas chambers as well as the barracks for the Sonderkommando prisoners and a field of mass graves. The entire SS contingent consisted of only 20-25 Germans with about 120 guards from the training camp in Trawniki. In December 1942 transports stopped coming to the camp. From January to April 1943 the corpses of the murdered were burnt to remove any evidence of what had taken place here. There was no proper crematorium in the camp. The corpses of the victims were burnt on primitive grates made from railway sleepers. The stench of the burning bodies could be smelt even at a distance of 25 kilometres from Bełżec. Between April and June 1943 all the buildings in the camp were destroyed and the last prisoners made up of Sonderkommando squads were transported by the Germans to Sobibor where they were murdered. Bełżec camp ceased to exist. It is known that only three prisoners survived Bełżec camp and were able to testify after the war. In a very short time Bełżec became the most forgotten extermination camp, although its existence was common knowledge in occupied Poland. It was only in 1963 that the first monument was erected in the area of the former camp. It, however, was not informative enough about the way the genocide had been committed in the camp. The camp area lay forsaken and forgotten for many years. In 1993 an agreement between the American Jewish Committee and the Polish government was signed for the erection of a new monument and the creation of a museum in the area of the former camp. This construction work, as such, was preceded by an archeological dig. Between 2002 and 2004 a complex of monuments was built within the territory which covered most of the former camp. The creators of these monuments were Andrzej Sołyga, Zdzisław Pidek and Marcin Roszczyk. The idea they had was to commemorate the victims of the camp by presenting Bełżec as one, vast burial ground. When working on the project, they were aware that they had to show appropriate and fitting respect for the traditions of Judaism. Together with the monuments a museum was created to house an exhibition devoted to the history of the extermination camp in Bełżec against the background of occupied Poland. On June 3, 2004 the complex was officially opened and since has been known as, Muzeum-Miejsce Pamięci w Bełżcu, Oddział Państwowego Muzeum na Majdanku (The Bełżec Museum and Memorial a part of the National Museum in Majdanek)

Belzec

Gypsy children from the Bełżec labour camp. Before the extermination camp was created in the spring of 1940 the Germans created a labour camp in which about 7000 Jewish men from the area of the General Government as well as several thousand Polish Gypsies – the Roma and over 2000 German Gypsies – the Sinti and several hundred Poles were imprisoned. The prisoners were forced to dig a tank trap along the border with the Soviet Union. The labour camp functioned from the autumn of 1940 and had its sub-camps in Lipsk, Płaszów and Cieszanów. Conditions here were very primitive. Several hundred Jews, Roma and Sinti either died of hunger or infectious diseases or were shot by the Germans. Among the victims were many Gypsy children who did not work and thus did not receive any food rations. Two massive 'Gypsy graves' are preserved today in Bełżec. They are situated in the former manor house park near the road from Bełżec to Jarosław (photography taken in 1940).

The train station in Bełżec. All the transports that came to the camp between March and December 1942 stopped here. There were days when several transports with Jewish deportees stopped at the station waiting to enter the camp. Some of the prisoners tried to escape from the transport at the station. Most of them were shot as they tried to flee. This all happened in front of people waiting for the passenger trains. The train station was destroyed in July 1944 during a Soviet air raid on Bełżec. All the railway documentation concerning the camp was lost when the station was bombed (view before 1944).

Jewish prisoners from the Sonderkommando in Bełżec extermination camp. One of the few photographs taken inside the camp. Taking pictures of the camp was strictly forbidden by order of the camp authorities. The members of Sonderkommando, about 500 prisoners, were usually men and, in the latter period, women. Their main task was to work inside the camp. A special group of prisoners were used for work inside the gas chambers. They moved the corpses out of the gas chambers and buried them in the mass graves. The prisoners in this group were the ones who were replaced the most often. After a few days of this work they were so exhausted they were shot and replaced by new prisoners from the newly arrived transports. Other Sonderkommando prisoners were responsible for segregating the property of the exterminated or acted as servants to the German camp guards. Women worked in the prison laundry, in the canteen for the guards and the camp headquarters (photograph taken probably in 1942).

The extermination camp in Bełżec was demolished by the Germans between April and June 1943.
All the buildings were painstakingly destroyed. The mass graves were leveled and trees planted on them.
In the immediate post war period the area was ransacked by grave robbers looking for gold and valuables.
The first monument to be erected was in 1963 (photograph taken in 1945).

← Rudolf Kamm, a SS German guard in front of the camp barracks. The SS contingency consisted of between 20
and 25 Germans, officers and non-commissioned officers, and 120 guards, former war prisoners from the Soviet Union
who went over to the side of the Germans. Among the guards were Ukrainians from central and eastern Ukraine,
Russians and Volga Germans. All of them were characterized by their extreme brutality towards the prisoners.
After the war only 8 Germans were tried for crimes of genocide committed in Bełżec. Only one of them was found guilty.
He was sentenced to 5 years in prison. More guards from Bełżec were tried in the Soviet Union after the war.
Some of them were sentenced to death (photograph probably taken in 1942).

A part of the exhibition in the Bełżec Memorial.
The new museum was opened officially on June 3, 2004.
The monument and the exhibition are a part of the Polish-American Project. At the permanent Bełżec exhibition visitors can learn about the history of the camp, the Holocaust, its victims and the perpetrators of this crime. Numerous exhibits related to the history of the camp can be also found in the museum (contemporary photograph).

Nisza-Ohel, a part of the new monument in Bełżec.
The names of the victims are engraved on the stone plaques.
The overwhelming majority of the Jews murdered in Bełżec have never been identified. No record of their identity was ever kept. The names engraved in Nisza come from the archives of the towns and villages whose inhabitants were deported to Bełżec extermination camp between March 17 and the middle of December 1942 (contemporary photograph).

A symbolic ramp with a pile of railway sleepers, commemorating the deportation and the stacks of wood on which from April 1943 the Germans burnt the corpses of those murdered in the gas chambers (contemporary photograph).

View of the Museum grounds – mass graves and the names → of the victims who between March 17 and the middle of December 1942 were deported here. Around the monument are over 260 names of the locations from which the prisoners were deported. They include towns and villages from the pre-war territory of Poland and over 40 places in Germany, Austria, the Czech Republik and Slovakia (contemporary photograph).

The Nazi, German extermination camp in Sobibór (SS-Sonderkommando Sobibor) was in operational use in the period between May 1942 and October 1943. The first transports of Jews arrived in Sobibór at the end of April 1942. The vast majority of the newly transported were selected for immediate extermination. Only a few people were selected to work in the different 'kommando' groups in the area of the camp. The number of Sobibór victims is estimated at around 250 thousand people. They were mostly Jews from: Poland, Germany, Austria, the Czech Republik, Slovakia, France, the Netherlands, Romania, Hungary, Belgium and the occupied territory of the Soviet Union, mainly Belarus. Approximately one thousand Poles were also murdered in the camp. The decision to build an extermination camp in Sobibór was made most probably in February 1942 after the conference on 'the Final Solution of the Jewish Question' organized January 20, 1942 in Wannsee near Berlin by Reinhard Heydrich and Adolf Eichmann. The building of the camp known in the official nomenclature as 'SS-Sonderkommando Sobibor' commenced in March 1942. The construction was supervised by the head of the SS Construction Office and Police in Zamość who later became the first Commandant of the camp – Richard Thomalla. Some 58 hectares (143 acres) of forest on the left side of the Chełm-Włodawa railway line were cleared for the use of the camp. At the end of April 1942 the entire area of the camp was fenced off by a triple row of barbed wire 2.5 meters (8 feet) high, camouflaged on the outside with fir tree branches. Watchtowers were placed along the length of the entire fence and in 1943 the Germans additionally placed minefields around the camp. The camp buildings in Sobibór constituted a few separate complexes of buildings (the outskirts of the camp, Camps I, II, III and IV).

Each part of the Sobibór camp was surrounded by an additional inner barbed wire fence forming an inner, isolated entity. The 'Way of Death' was the road which curved from Camp II to Camp III – the place of immediate extermination and it was well guarded. The camp prisoners named the road 'the snake' and the Germans called it, the 'Road to Heaven'. Both the SS and the conscripted guards took part in the unloading of people from the wagons and guarding their movement. These proceedings always followed the same routine and had one objective, the extermination of the people as soon as they arrived. The transport was divided up into parts and three or four wagons were pulled to the unloading ramp. The camp gate was then closed. The old, the sick and the disabled were loaded onto the camp's railway flat cars (the SS guards wore Red Cross armbands) and were told that they were to be taken to a field hospital. In reality they were shot in the camp by a firing squad. After selection according to sex and age made on the ramp the other prisoners were escorted in a single file to the area of Camp II. From here people, naked and divided into groups of 50 to 100, were taken to the gas chambers. Women were escorted through the connecting barracks where they had their hair cut short by a group of 'hairdressers'. The gas chambers were designed and painted so as to resemble real bath houses. In the beginning, 240 people could be gassed at once. After the building was extended this capacity was doubled. The victims were asphyxiated by exhaust fumes supplied to the chamber from a special annex in which an 8 cylinder diesel engine was situated. The extermination process lasted around 15-20 minutes. After the process of gassing was completed the corpses were carried out of the chambers and searched for gold and hidden valuables. The corpses were then thrown into the huge mass graves in the area of Camp III. From the autumn of 1942 the corpses were burnt on special wooden stacks made from railway sleepers. Corpses were placed in layers between the wooden sleepers, soaked with any kind of inflammable liquid, and then set on fire. The ashes were thrown into pits in the area of Camp III. On October 14, 1943 an armed uprising of prisoners broke out in the camp. Its leaders were Aleksander Peczerski and Leon Feldhendler. The rebellion ended with a massive break out of prisoners with about 300 people escaping from the camp. Many of them, however, were recaptured and shot by the Germans. Only about 50 escapees survived the war. It is thanks to them that those guilty of the murders in the camp were tried and the truth about the camp at Sobibór came to light. The success of the armed uprising compelled the Germans to close down the camp immediately and they tried to hide all the traces of genocide at the site. The camp was closed down very quickly. The gas chambers were blown up and the barracks and fences dismantled. Rubble and other building materials left after the demolition were removed and hidden. A pine forest was planted in the area of the former camp. The idea of commemorating the victims murdered in this Nazi camp of direct extermination in Sobibór was put forward in the mid 1960's as an initiative of the Polish 'Rada Ochrony Pamięci Walk I Męczeństwa' (the Committee for Safeguarding Monuments of Struggle and Martyrdom) The place of extermination was commemorated by a burial mound – a mausoleum containing the ashes of the murdered people and a monument. The Museum at the Former Nazi Death Camp in Sobibór on the terrain of the camp has been open since 1993. The museum is a part of the Museum of the Łęczyn-Włodawa Lake District in Włodawa.

Sobibor

The model of the German extermination camp in Sobibór made by Aleksander Pac, engineer, on the basis
of the plans by Thomas Blatt. For a better understanding the buildings are disproportionately large compared to the area.
The model of Sobibor is a permanent exhibit in the Museum of the Holocaust in Los Angeles.

Od 10 marca znowu jest czynny obóz śmierci w Sobiborze. Przywożą tam teraz Żydów z Holandii i Francji. Żydzi ci jadą w osobowych wagonach i są przekonani, że wiozą ich na roboty do fabryk przemysłu wojennego na Wschodzie. W niedzielę 14 marca Żydów holenderskich witano w Sobiborze nawet orkiestrą, na drugi dzień już żadnego z nich nie było przy życiu.

Informacja Bieżąca Nr 13 z 1IV 1943 r.

Dokument wywiadu Delegatury Rządu RP na Kraj o transportach Żydów holenderskich i francuskich.

From March 10 the extermination camp in Sobibór is once more operational. Jews from the Netherlands and France are transported here. They are transported in separate wagons and think they are being taken to the war industry factories in the East. On Sunday March 14, Dutch Jews were welcomed to Sobibór by an orchestra, the next day not one of them were alive. Current information number 13 from April 1, 1943 – intelligence document from the delegation of the Government of the Republic of Poland for the situation in the country concerning the transport of Dutch and French Jews.

51

On October 14, 1943 an armed uprising broke out in the camp. Its leaders were
Aleksander Peczerski and Leon Feldhendler.

The insurgents at Sobibór. Upper row: Fiszel Bialowicz, Jakub Biskubicz, Thomas Blatt, Hersz Cukierman, Josef Duniec, Chaim Engel, Selma Wijnberg-Engel, Hela Weiss; middle row: Berl Freiberg, Mosze Goldfarb, Chaim Lejst, Samuel Lerer, Jehuda Lerner, Eda Fiszer-Lichtman, Ichak Lichtman, Abraham Margules; bottom row: Zelda Metz-Kelberman, Chaim Powroznik, Ester Turner-Raab, Siemion Rosenfeld, Azyk Rottenberg, Moshe Bahir, Szlomo Szmajzner, Kurt Thomas-Ticho. The uprising ended with a massive escape of prisoners. All together about 300 prisoners escaped from the camp. Many of them were recaptured and shot by the Germans.

Franz Stagl – the Commandant of Treblinka and Sobibór camps.
The confrontation with a survivor in a Brazilian Court, 1967.

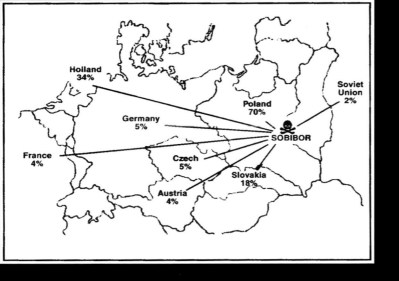

Main routes of transport of Jews to Sobibór between May 1942 and September 1943.

Memorial wall commemorating the victims of the camp at Sobibór with commemorative inscriptions in Jewish, Hebrew, Yiddish, English, Dutch, French, German and Slovak (contemporary photograph).

Female prisoner with child – the monument commemorating the victims of Sobibór standing in the area of the camp (contemporary photograph by Mieczysław Welter).

The Treblinka extermination camp was built by the Germans next to an existing penal labour camp in the middle of 1942. The camp covered 17 hectares (42 acres). It was surrounded by a high barbed wire fence to hide from outside what was happening inside the camp. The Germans even wove tree branches into the barbed wire as camouflage. Anti-tank obstacles were placed together with coils of barbed wire on the outside of the fence. Watchtowers were also built in different parts of the camp. The camp guard force consisted of 25-30 Germans and Austrians who managed the camp and a company of guards, about 100 men, mainly of Ukrainian origin. Doctor Irmfried Eberl was appointed the Commandant of the camp. The post was then taken over by Franz Stangl. His deputy was Kurt Franz. The first transport of deported people came to the camp on July 23, 1942. It brought Jews from the Warsaw Ghetto. Up until then Jews from occupied Poland, the Czech Republik, Slovakia, France, Greece, Yugoslavia, the Soviet Union, Germany and Austria were transported here. Some transports also included Roma Gypsies from Poland and Germany. These people were killed using exhaust fumes in specially built gas chambers. It is estimated that over 800 thousand people were exterminated in Treblinka. To hide the traces of this genocide the corpses were burned on specially constructed stacks of wood. On August 2, 1943 an armed uprising broke out in the camp. From 840 prisoners only about 200 managed to escape from the camp and from that number only about 100 survived the war. After the uprising the Germans decided to gradually demolish the camp.

In November 1943 all the camp structures and installations were destroyed. The Germans built a house for a Ukrainian family on the site and the area around it was ploughed and planted with lupine. When the Russian Army was close the house and buildings were burnt down. After the war there were cases of profanation of the site. It was only in the nineteen fifties that three artists-professors: Adam Haupt, Franciszek Duszenko and Franciszek Strynkiewicz created a team and were successful in preparing the layout of a new project to commemorate those murdered in the former camp. They did not limit their idea to a mere memorial but took into account the whole area. The borders of the former camp were demarcated by gigantic granite columns. The main gate was marked by two blocks of concrete between which lay a cobbled road leading to the ramp. The concrete blocks on the way to the ramp symbolize the railway tracks and were an idea by Adam Haupt. Next to the ramp are ten rocks with the names of the countries from which the Jews were transported to the camp and a paved road going from the ramp to the monument. This uphill road led to the gas chambers and was called, 'the Road to Heaven'. On both sides were changing rooms, now marked by the rocks, on the left a changing room for women, on the right for men. In the place where the gas chambers once stood is a tall monument, by Franciszek Duszenko. It was made from huge granite blocks and its design resembles the 'Wailing Wall' in Jerusalem. It has a huge vertical break in the centre. The upper part of the monument is a finished finial on whose west side is a mural presenting human remains and the blessing hands – symbols taken from Jewish tombstones. On the east side of the monument there is a menorah, the symbol of Judaism. In front of the monument is an inscription reading, 'NEVER AGAIN' in Polish, Hebrew, Yiddish, Russian, English, French and German. The memorial is the symbolic grave of all the victims of Treblinka. Behind the monument there is a rectangular hollow – representing the place where corpses were burnt. It is a rectangular pit filled with melted black basalt forming irregular coagula and icicle-like shapes. Around the pit there are more than a dozen petroleum lamps which, when lit, reminds visitors that in a place like this corpses were burnt. The idea for this monument came from Adam Haupt. About 22 thousand square meters (5.5 acres) of the camp were covered with concrete with 17 thousand granite blocks fixed in it. The blocks symbolize Jewish tombstones. On 216 of them the names of the locations from which the murdered Jews were transported are carved. One granite block is a memorial to Janusz Korczak (Henryk Goldszmit) and the children from his orphanage who were murdered in Treblinka. It is the only 'gravestone' with a name on it. The entire area is unadorned and bleak. The grayness of the concrete and granite remind visitors of the more than 800 thousand people whose ashes were scattered across this huge area. From 1983 the territory of the former camp, the sand and gravel pit, 'the Black Road' and the area around the camp became the Museum of Struggle and Martyrdom in Treblinka, a part of the Regional Museum in Siedlce.

Treblinka

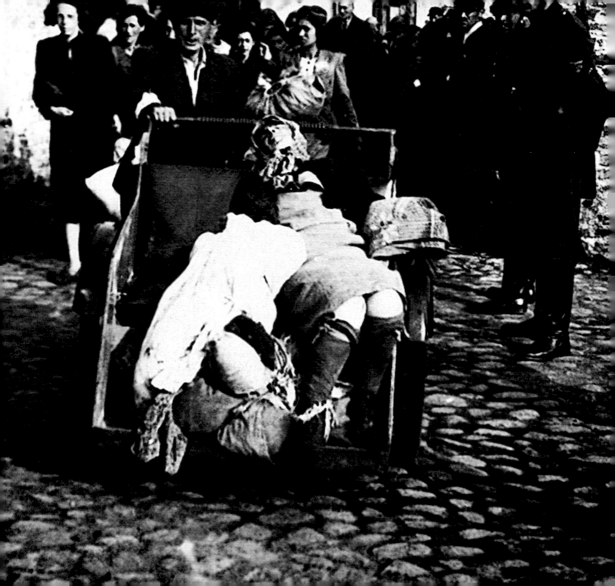

Jews waiting for transport to Treblinka at the Umschlagplatz, Warsaw – the former square on Stawki Street, connected to the Gdański railway station by the station siding (photograph taken in 1942).

Jews being forced into wagons at Umschlagplatz. From 2 to 13.5 thousand people were transported to Treblinka every day (photograph taken in 1942).

← Umschlagplatz – in an area of approximately 2.4 thousand square meters (0.6 acres) some 10 thousand Jews were kept waiting with neither food nor water for many hours (photography taken in 1942).

German information sign at the village of Treblinka, situated near the extermination camp
(photograph taken between 1939 and 1945).

The camp ablaze after the uprising. The photograph was taken on August 2, 1943 by a worker
at the train station Treblinka – about 6 kilometres (3.7 miles) from the camp.

The Treblinka extermination camp after the war. Between 1944 and 1959 the camp was not commemorated. →
or protected in any way. Traces of genocide – scattered human remains (photography taken after the war).

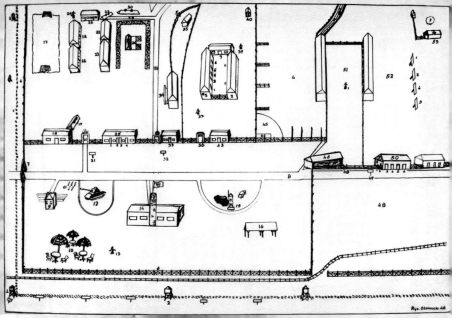

Rys. Oksmuski 46

The first committee examining the area of the camp (photograph taken after the war).

In the area of the mass graves a symbolic cemetery of 17 thousand rocks was created in memory of those murdered in Treblinka (contemporary photograph).

The concentration camp in Lublin was named Majdanek after a district of Lublin called Majdan Tatarski, which was close to the camp. The camp functioned from October 1941 to June 1944. The decision to create it was made by SS Reichsführer Heinrich Himmler in June 1941, a month after the Red Army invaded the eastern part of Poland. The decision itself was also a consequence of the III Reich plans to create more 'living space' for the German race. The agricultural region around Lublin was to be base for the economy and the camp was to be a source of labour. The camp was to have many other functions. It was to be a place of Jewish extermination, a concentration camp for political prisoners and a prison camp for prisoners of war from the Soviet Union. The Nazis used their doctrine of collective responsibility where hundreds or even entire communities could be killed in retaliation for an act of resistance. Some of the victims of this doctrine were sent to this camp. It was also to serve as a temporary camp for displaced people. Its creation was undertaken by the chief of the SS and Police in the Lublin district, Odilo Globocnik. Some 270 hectares (approx. 665 acres) of land to the south-east of Lublin, next to the Zamość-Lwów road was reserved for the camp. Between 1941 and 1944 the Central SS Construction Office and Police in Lublin built the camp which was comprised of a prison, administrative office and farming areas. About 280 different buildings were created. The prison part included five rectangular fields (the clearing of the sixth was stopped) and two 'interfields' i.e. stripes of land between Fields I and II as well as between Fields IV and V. In each field there were two rows of primitive, wooden barracks. In Fields I, II and V there were barracks with windows, in Fields III and IV barracks of a farm stable type without any windows were put up. The middle of the field was made up of the assembly square with a gallows in the middle. The first interfield contained the laundry and the 'small crematorium' with two furnaces burning

lowgrade oil, the second a coal storage area. The prison fields were surrounded by double rows of barbed wire with watchtowers and guards at the gates. A strip of land called 'the Death Zone' was created on the inner side of the fenced fields. Anyone who entered this zone was shot immediately. In 1942 in Field I three gas chambers were built and adapted for the use of Zyklon B and carbon monoxide. In 1943 behind Field V a new crematorium, designed by the German company K. Kori, was built with 5 furnaces fired by coke. The farming area grew mostly vegetables but also contained barracks in the western sector of the prison fields, with storage sheds and maintenance-production workshops. On the outskirts were the barracks and living quarters for the guards and the Commandant. Over a period of less than three years during which time the camp was operational five Commandants administered the camp. They were: Karl Otto Koch, Max Koegel, Hermann Florstedt, Martin Weiss and Arthur Liebehenschel. The head overseer of the women's camp during its entire existence (1942-1944) was Elsa Ehrich. The head overseer of the crematoria was Erich Muhsfeldt. Those held in Majdanek were a mixture of people, of different denominations, political views, social positions and professions, both members of a nation's elite and more ordinary, simple folk. The population of the camp was made up of people from about 30 different countries. Polish citizens were the dominant group (mainly Jews and Poles) but there were also citizens of the Soviet Union, the Czech Republik and Slovakia. Citizens of other nations made a small percentage of the imprisoned. The largest ethnic group were the Jews (deported mainly from Poland, Austria, Germany, the Czech Republik, Slovakia, the Netherlands and France), Poles, Russians, Byelorussians and Ukrainians. They were not only men and women but also children transported together with their families. The average population of the camp varied from 10 thousand to 15 thousand, and only in the summer of 1943 did it reach 24 thousand. A characteristic of Majdanek was the large percentage of people from rural areas deported from the Zamość region and the pacified Byelorussian villages and transported to Majdanek. The camp was notorious for its extremely primitive, unsanitary living conditions. Food rations were kept at a minimum, a sewage system was installed only in 1943. Starvation and dirt led to many diseases spreading across the camp which was the cause of the high death rate among those imprisoned. According to the official German statistics from August 1943 Majdanek had the highest death rate of all the concentration camps. People died of starvation, cold, disease, exhaustion, brutal treatment, overwork, torture, a complex system of punishments, harassment and straight forward, unpremeditated murder. The largest execution took place on November 3, 1943 as part of the 'Erntfest Aktion' (operation harvest) when around 18 thousand Jews from Majdanek and labour camps in Lublin were shot in the ditches dug behind Field V.

The few documents in existence today do not allow for an estimate of the exact number of victims from Majdanek. The latest research suggests that around 150,000 people entered the camp, of which nearly 80,000 died. Among these were around 60,000 Jews and 20,000 inmates of other natonalities, mainly Poles, Russians and Byelorussians. The camp ceased to function on July 23rd 1944. In November 1944 the National Museum of Majdanek was created and was the first of its kind and covered a third of the territory of the former camp and contained the most important traces of buildings in the camp.

In 1969 to commemorate the victims of Majdanek the Memorial of Struggle and Martyrdom was erected. The monument was by Wiktor Tołkin and is in the form of a stylized gate. The monument is connected to the Mausoleum by the 'Way of Homage'. Under the dome of the Mausoleum are the ashes of those murdered in the camp.

Majdanek

Construction work in the area of the camp. On the right is the extension of barrack 41 in which
the bath house was situated. A gas chamber bunker is visible under the wooden shed. One of the 18 watchtowers can
be seen on the left (photography from 1943).

The farm part of the camp. On the right are storage houses with the belongings robbed from the inmates and supply
materials of various kinds. On the left, maintenance-production workshops (photography taken in 1943).

Prisoners were forced to do hard labour during the construction of the camp and the transport of building materials. The barracks of the soldiers who guarded the camp are in the background (photography taken in 1943).

The fence around the prison part of the camp constructed in the form of a 'crow's nest'. To prevent escape high voltage wire was fixed to the angled poles between the two rows of regular wire (photography taken in the fifties).

The inside of a prison barrack. Each was built to contain 250 people but they were often very overcrowded with prisoners. In the early days of the camp the prisoners slept on the ground. Eventually three level bunks were installed to accommodate even more prisoners (photograph taken in the fifties).

Stable type barracks in Field III (male field). This was called the 'Death Field' because of the horrendous and extreme conditions the prisoners lived under (photograph taken in the fifties).

The inside of a bath house. For the SS the baths were another opportunity to torment the prisoners (photograph taken in the fifties).

The Three Eagles Column in Field III made in 1943 by the prisoners from a project by one of the prisoners, Albin Maria Boniecki. Ashes of murdered victims were secretly placed in the base of the column (photography taken in 1962).

An aerial view of the camp from the west. In the foreground the camp vegetable garden, in the centre →
the potato storage sheds, farm barracks and Field I (photograph taken in 1944).

The crematorium built behind Field V
in the second half of 1943 with a complex
of five furnaces fueled by coke. Ashes from
the crematorium's victims were used
to fertilise the camp farm fields.
Numerous executions were carried out
inside the crematorium and around it.
Those murdered were camp prisoners
and prisoners from the Nazi prison
in the Castle in Lublin. Executions were
particularly frequent at the beginning of 1944
(photography taken in the early fifties).

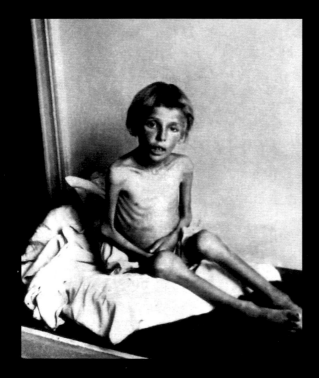

One of the children from Zamość region – Ania Rempa. During the mass pacification-deportation action in July 1943 she was deported with her family from the village of Zawadka in the district of Biłgoraj and sent to Majdanek. She was freed in such a state of ill health that she died in hospital a month later (photography taken in 1943).

← The crematorium furnaces after the crematorium had been set on fire in July 22, 1944 by the camp guards who were fleeing the camp. In front of the furnaces the remains of the corpses of the victims of the last executions (photography from 1944).

The Mausoleum with the ashes of the murdered victims. The inscription frieze reads: 'Let our fate
be a warning to you'. In the foreground stands a rock with a plaque commemorating the mass execution of Jews
on November, 3 1943 (contemporary photograph).

Field III contains the only remaining prison barracks. In other fields washing troughs installed
in 1943 can be seen (contemporary photograph).

Shoes belonging to the victims of Majdanek and those murdered around the Lublin District. →
A part of 'Operation Reinhardt' (contemporary photograph).

The Chełmno extermination camp was the first German Nazi death camp in which Jews were murdered on a massive scale. It began to function on December 8, 1941. A small village in Greater Poland was chosen for this centre for Jewish extermination. Chełmno-on-Ner was situated not far from the town of Koło which had good railway and road connections to Łódź, the biggest Jewish centre in the 'Reichsgau Wartheland' ('Land of the Warta River'). This name was given to the area of Greater Poland annexed to the III Reich and included parts of the Warszawskie, Łódzkie and Pomorskie voivodships. The creation of the camp in Chełmno was preceded by the execution of Jews in the forests near Konin. The Jews were gassed in gas-vans, shot in the head or murdered in a particularly cruel way – thrown into a lime filled pit into which water was poured. This was undertaken by special Sonderkommando squads who became the guards in the Chełmno extermination camp. The activity of this camp can be divided into two periods.

The first period.
December 8, 1941, the first transport of prisoners from Koło arrived at the camp on April 11, 1943 the Sonderkommando left Chełmno. The extermination camp consisted of two parts: the burial grounds in a clearing of the Rzuchów forest about 4 kilometres (2.5 miles) from Chełmno and the estate with park and palace (blown up by the Germans, April 7, 1943) on the outskirts of the village. In the palace, the victims, on the pretext of disinfection, were forced to undress and go into the cellar and along a passageway to the specially designed gas-vans. The first victims were Jews from the ghetto in Koło and the surrounding area. The next victims were nearly 4 thousand Gypsies or Jews from the ghetto in Łódź, from Germany, Austria, the Czech Republic and Slovakia. The victim's bodies were buried in mass graves in the Rzuchów forest. In the summer of 1942 transports were stopped because the decomposing corpses were posing a serious danger of epidemic. The Germans then started to remove the corpses. They built four primitive furnaces in the grounds to burn the bodies. The death camp in Chełmno became a place of experimentation on corpse disposal. Initially, the Germans wanted to dissolve the corpses in lime. When this method proved to be ineffective there were attempts to get rid of bodies by means of explosives. Finally, the Germans decided to burn the bodies in furnaces which had been built in the grounds. It was only in the autumn of 1942 with a massive amount of bodies to burn that two crematoria were built with chimneys visible over the tops of the trees in the forest. After cremation the remaining bones were ground down in a petrol engine driven grinder and the ashes scattered in the forest or thrown into one of the 11 ditches dug in a row beside the mass graves. For half a century it was thought that the palace was blown up because the Germans wanted to hide the traces of the genocide in the camp. Only after a proper investigation supported by the testimony of the only surviving witness was it understood that the Germans blew up the palace to kill a group of sick prisoners inside. They had been transported to the Chełmno camp shortly before the Sonderkommando left.

The second period
In the spring of 1944 the Sonderkommando came back to Chełmno. In one of the clearings in the Rzuchów forest two barracks were built which formed a temporary camp for the future victims. The way in which the prisoners were murdered was similar to that used in the first period. The church next to the landed estate was where the victims spent their last night before they were murdered. They were transported by van from the church to the forest. There they were told to strip because they were going to have a shower and then put into the gas-vans. The killings lasted from June 23 to July 1944 when 10 transports of Jews from Łódź arrived. The Chełmno extermination camp was too small and not functioning

efficiently at this time and most of the Jews from the liquidated Łódź ghetto were sent to KL Auschwitz. Only the members of the Sonderkommando and 47 prisoners – craftsmen who were imprisoned in the granary near the ruins of the castle remained in Chełmno. During the night of January 17 to 18, 1945 as the camp was being evacuated the last executions were carried out. The Germans led out their victims in groups of five and shot them in the back of the head. Those remaining fought back, killed two executioners and barricaded themselves in the granary. The Germans set the building on fire and the people inside were killed. Only two managed to escape. The question of how many people were murdered in the Chełmno extermination camp is particularly difficult to answer. According to post war estimates the numbers vary between 350 and 360 thousand. At present it is assumed that from 150 to 200 thousand people were exterminated in the camp. Between 1997 and 2005 through the initiative of the Polish 'Rada Ochrony Pamięci Walk I Męczeństwa' (the Committee for Safeguarding Monuments of Struggle and Martyrdom) a scientific and archeological study was carried out in the area of the camp. The investigations answered some of the questions about the functioning of the camp and revealed the position of the crematoria and the mass graves. The ruins of the palace were excavated and some personal effects of the people murdered there were found. In 1987, by decision of the local governor of the Koninskie voivodship, the Museum of the Former Extermination Camp in Chełmno-on-Ner was created as a part of the Regional Museum in Konin. The museum was opened on June 17, 1990. A 'Memorial Wall' was unveiled also to which the families of the murdered people attached their memorial plaques. From 1992 monuments commemorating the victims of Bełchatów, Brzeziny, Gąbin and Łódź were erected along the road to the 'Memorial Wall'

Kulmhof am Ner

Transport of Jews to Chełmno, changing trains at Koło train station (photograph taken in 1942).

Powiercie – reloading the belongings of the victims. From Powiercie the Jews were driven to the mill in the nearby village of Zawadka where they spent the night before being taken to the palace in Chełmno and death in the gas-vans (photograph taken in 1942).

Transport of Jews from
the Koło train station to Powiercie
(photograph taken in 1942).

The dramatic text of an appeal written on December 1, 1944 probably by one of the last victims in Chełmno
– Izaak Sigelman. The sheet of paper was saved by the escapee – Mordek Żurawski.

The Rzuchów forest – aerial view taken by the Luftwaffe of the burial grounds in May 1942.

Identification tag from Stalag Luckenwalde III found during research in the camp – the property of Henryk Pfeffer, son of Moszek and Maria, maiden name Kupfer, born in Łódź on September 23, 1914. Rank of private in the army, he served with the 10th Regiment of Infantry in Góra Kalwaria. Taken prisoner on September 9, 1939 (contemporary photograph).

A small pendant representing Moses with part of the prayer, 'Shemah Israel' on the reverse side. The pendant probably belonged to a woman from Germany (contemporary photograph).

The cover of a silver cigarette case found in the area of the camp. It had been given as first prize to Józef Jakubowski for winning the gymkhana (a race with artificial obstacles) on his 'Sokół 600 – Gordon Bennet' bike on August 30, 1936 (contemporary photograph).

93

Probably a fragment of a brooch made in the Litzmannstadt ghetto, found during an archeological dig in Chełmno (on Hitler's orders Łódź became Litzmannstadt from 1940 to 1945) (contemporary photograph).

The foundations of the palace uncovered during the archeological dig. In the background the granary in which the last of the camp prisoners were murdered (contemporary photograph).

Monument by Józef Stasiński and Jerzy Buszkiewicz, unveiled on September 27, 1964. →
The massive block of concrete (6-7 meters high) (22 feet high) is supported by five pyramids.
On its side there is a presentation in relief of the martyrdom of the victims.
Next to it is written, 'Pamiętamy'. 'We will remember' (contemporary photograph).